S0-DZE-987

# EXPLORE THE WORLD

**LIFE SCIENCE**

# Gone Forever

LIZ HUYCK

## TABLE OF CONTENTS

PIONEER VALLEY EDUCATIONAL PRESS, INC

# WIPEOUT

The bright, sunny sky suddenly turned black. The sound of millions of flapping wings filled the air. That's what it was like when a flock of passenger pigeons passed overhead.

Long ago, one out of every four birds in North America was a passenger pigeon. They flew from forest to forest in **massive** flocks. There were so many passenger pigeons that people thought they would always fill the skies. But in 1914, the last one died in a Cincinnati zoo. The **species** is now gone forever.

Why did the passenger pigeon go **extinct**?

Earth is a crowded place. At this moment, 30 million species of living things share our planet. But there have been 30 *billion* species in our planet's history, and almost all died out long ago, never to return. What happened to them all?

No species lasts forever. (None has so far, anyway.) In nature, living things compete for **survival**, and sometimes a species that doesn't compete well will die off.

MORE TO EXPLORE

The **STELLER'S SEA COW** was last seen in 1768. About 13,000 years ago, they were common in the colder waters of the Pacific Ocean. The last group of sea cows was discovered near Alaska in 1741. They spent all day floating and eating seaweed. The slow-moving giants were hunted for their meat and skins until they went extinct.

The **SMALL MAURITIAN FLYING FOX** was last seen in the 1800s. These creatures searched for nectar at night and slept all day. Hundreds would crowd together in giant hollow trees. As forests were cut down, the flying fox died out too.

MORE TO EXPLORE

Most of the time, species go extinct at a slow rate. But sometimes, large numbers of species die quickly. Scientists call these wipeouts mass extinctions.

Mass extinctions happen when the earth changes in some sudden or dramatic way. Maybe a volcano erupts or two landforms drift together. The temperature might get much hotter or colder. Or maybe an **asteroid** crash-lands on Earth. When a large change like this happens, the plants and animals that can't cope may become extinct.

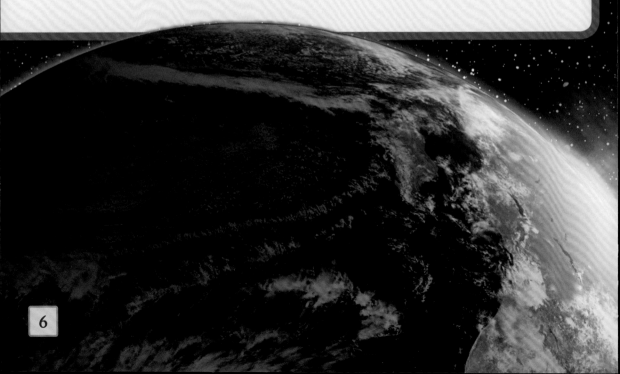

**38 million years ago** Moeritherium

**12–7 million years ago** Platybelodon

**1.8 million years ago** Mastodon

**400,000 years ago** Woolly Mammoth

The mass extinction that put an end to the dinosaurs occurred 65 million years ago. Many scientists believe it was caused when a giant asteroid struck the planet.

No mass extinctions have totally wiped out life on Earth. After each mass extinction, new species have taken the place of those that died. For example, the death of the dinosaurs made room in the world for mammals.

Present day

Indian Elephant

Present day

African Elephant

The passenger pigeon might also have been a victim of mass extinction, but not because of a killer asteroid or a natural disaster. They were killed by humans.

With their billion-bird flocks, passenger pigeons needed huge areas of wild forest for nesting and finding food. When the flock nested in a forest, every branch of every tree sagged under the weight of pigeon nests. Pigeon hunters blasted away underneath the trees, shooting all the pigeons they could. One hunter recalled bringing down 18 birds with a single shot from a shotgun.

At the same time, their forest homes were disappearing as people cut down trees for wood and expanded farms and cities. By the late 1800s, the birds were in trouble. Because females laid just one egg per year, there were not enough babies to take the place of all the birds being killed.

**The last wild passenger pigeon was shot in 1900.**

# OUR CHANGING WORLD

For many years, humans have been just one of the millions of species living on Earth. Over time, our population grew and grew and grew, and it's still growing. Scientists believe that in 50 years there will be twice as many humans living on Earth. That will take away even more food and space from other species.

# WORLD POPULATION
# 1950–2050

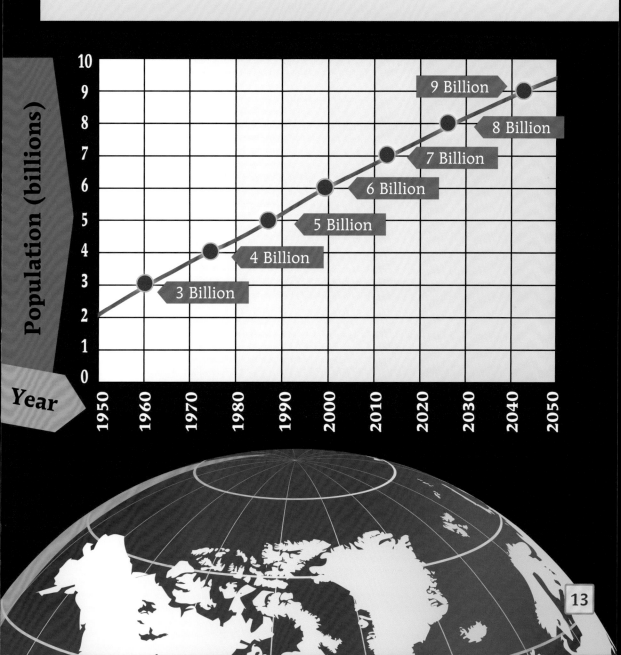

Population (billions)

10
9
8
7
6
5
4
3
2
1
0

9 Billion
8 Billion
7 Billion
6 Billion
5 Billion
4 Billion
3 Billion

Year

1950
1960
1970
1980
1990
2000
2010
2020
2030
2040
2050

13

Everywhere they go, people change the environment, cutting down forests and polluting streams and rivers. Because of these changes to their habitats, species are disappearing faster than any other time since the dinosaurs died out.

# THE SIXTH EXTINCTION

It's impossible to say exactly how many species have gone extinct recently or how many more will go extinct in the future. Scientists haven't even identified all of the world's creatures yet. We know that birds and amphibians have been hit hardest. One out of every three frog species is threatened with extinction. But mammals, fish, insects, and plants are also at risk.

MORE TO EXPLORE

Scientists are working to protect the **AMAZON RAIN FOREST**. This area is home to many different animals, plants, and insects.

Scientists are also working to protect **AUSTRALIA'S GREAT BARRIER REEF.** This area is home to many endangered fish. Half of the reef is now considered dead or dying.

More animals are going extinct now than ever before. If extinction continues at this rapid pace, half the species on Earth may disappear in the next 100 years. This would become the sixth mass extinction in our planet's history. If that happens, it would take millions of years for new species to take their place.

Extinction is a part of life. Without it, humans and the animals and plants we love might never have had their chance. But what will the world look like with half of its species gone? What will the world be like after we've said goodbye to prairie dogs, polar bears, bluefin tunas, and African black rhinos? Do we really want to find out?

bluefin tuna

# a COMEBACK

WE ARE WORKING to bring these ancient creatures back from the brink of extinction by creating safer fishing methods and protecting beaches where mother sea turtles can safely lay their eggs. Of the seven different species of sea turtle, only one is endangered now.

polar bear

prairie dog

African black rhinoceros

# GLOSSARY

**asteroid**

a rock in outer space that circles around the sun

**extinct**

no longer existing

**massive**

large

**species**

a group of animals or plants that are similar

**survival**

staying alive

# SEA TURTLES MAKE

SEA TURTLES are one of the oldest creatures living on Earth. These large, slow-moving reptiles have swum in our oceans for more than 110 million years but recently have faced an uncertain future. With people illegally hunting them, fishing nets accidentally catching them, and their habitats being polluted or taken over by people, sea turtles are struggling to stay alive. The good news is that efforts to save these egg-laying creatures are paying off.

# EXPLORE

## Level Q

Fairy-Tale Sci

From Wolf to

Gone Fore

Say What, H

**Pick three words** from the index to write about why some animals have become extinct. Underline each word that you use from the index.

Adapted from "Gone Forever," written by Liz Huy and published in *Ask Magazine* July 2006 © by Carus Publish

All Cricket Media material is copyrighted by Carus Publishing Com and illustrators. Any commercial use or distribution of mater Please visit cricketmedia.com/licensing for licensing an

EARTH SCIENCE

LIFE SCIENCE

PHYSICAL SCIENCE

SOCIAL SCIENCE

# EXPLORE THE WORLD

## PIONEER VALLEY **BOOKS**

pioneervalleybooks.com

## Gone Forever

LEVEL Q

ISBN 978-1-60343-216-0

9 781603 432160

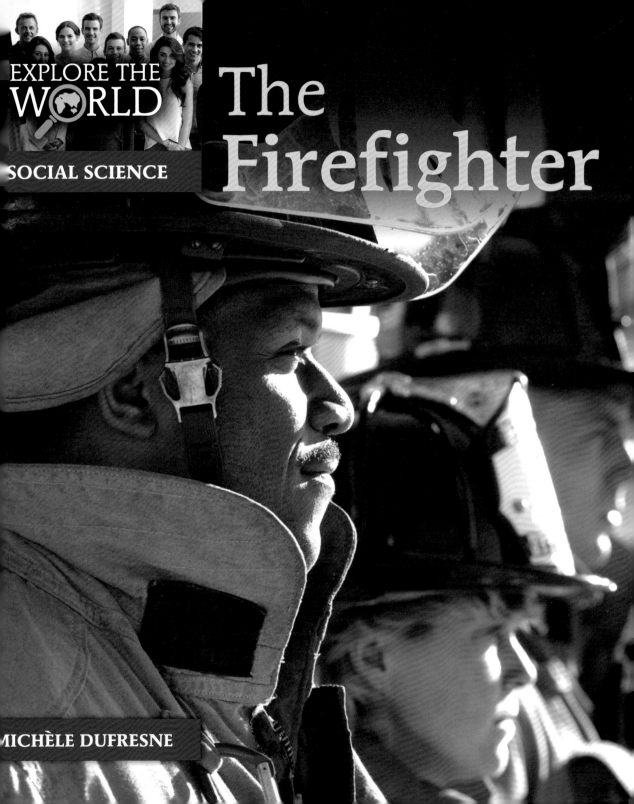

# EXPLORE THE WORLD

## SOCIAL SCIENCE

# The Firefighter

MICHÈLE DUFRESNE

Firefighters need
special equipment
to stay safe and
to do their job. Let's
read about what
a firefighter needs
to do his or her job.

terstock

y be reproduced, stored in a retrieval
ns, electronic, mechanical, photocopying,
permission of the publisher.